The Path of Love

Also by Becca Stevens

Walking Bible Study:
The Path of Peace

Walking Bible Study:
The Path of Justice

Funeral for a Stranger:
Thoughts on Life and Love

Hither & Yon:
A Travel Guide for the Spiritual Journey

Sanctuary:
Unexpected Places Where God Found Me

Find Your Way Home:
Words from the Street, Wisdom from the Heart
by the Women of Magdalene
with an introduction by Becca Stevens

BECCA STEVENS

Walking Bible Study

The Path of Love

ABINGDON PRESS / Nashville

Walking Bible Study
The Path of Love

Copyright © 2010 by Abingdon Press

All rights reserved. Except as stated elsewhere, all rights on all material are reserved by Abingdon Press and no part of this work may be reproduced or transmitted in any form or by any means, electronic or mechanical, including photocopying and recording, or by any information storage or retrieval system, except as may be expressly permitted by the 1976 Copyright Act or in writing from the publisher. Permission requests should be addressed to Permissions Office, 201 8th Avenue South, Nashville, TN 37203; permissions@abingdonpress.com.

This book is printed on acid-free, recycled paper.

Library of Congress Cataloging-in-Publication Data

Stevens, Becca, 1963-
  Walking Bible study / Becca Stevens.
      p. cm.
  ISBN 978-1-4267-1174-9 (v. 3 : alk. paper)
  1. Bible—Devotional literature. 2. Nature—Religious aspects—Christianity. I. Title.
  BS491.5.S78 2010
  220.071—dc22

                                                              2010022231

Scripture quotations, unless otherwise indicated, are from the New Revised Standard Version of the Bible, copyright © 1989 by the Division of Christian Education of the National Council of Churches of Christ in the United States of America, and are used by permission.

Scripture quotations marked (NIV) are taken from the HOLY BIBLE, NEW INTERNATIONAL VERSION®. NIV®. Copyright © 1973, 1978, 1984 by International Bible Society. Used by permission of Zondervan Publishing House. All rights reserved.

Scripture quotations marked (NKJV) are taken from the New King James Version. Copyright © 1982 by Thomas Nelson, Inc. Used by permission. All rights reserved.

10 11 12 13 14 15 16 17 18 19 — 10 9 8 7 6 5 4 3 2 1

MANUFACTURED IN THE UNITED STATES OF AMERICA

It may not be right to dedicate a book to wild-flowers, but some of them changed my life and grew my faith. I am especially grateful to the sweet clover that taught me in my own backyard to see the beauty of the earth, that allowed me to make crowns for my head when I needed to feel beautiful, and that filled my imagination with their peaceful scent. I am forever grateful.

————————————

I would like to thank Marcus Hummon, Levi, Caney, and Moses for teaching me how much fun the woods and a river are.

Table of Contents

The Path of Love / 9
Using This Book / 11
Walking Bible Study / 13

Pear Blossoms for Sadie

Week 1. The Creator's Vision / 21
Meditations

Week 2. Moses' Vision / 37
Meditations

Week 3. Mark's Vision / 57
Meditations

Week 4. Paul's Vision / 75
Meditations

I Lay Me Down in Flowers

The Path of Love

Welcome to Walking Bible Study, a series of short readings and meditations inviting you into nature and along the many paths to God.

As in life, the walk can be taken alone, with a spouse or friend, or in a group. You can journey up a mountain, into the woods, around the block, or to the flowers in your window box. Wherever you choose to go, remember that the Kingdom is not a place we are headed to, but a place we live in as we walk with God.

In this book we follow the path of love, a path begun when God created the world from two chaotic elements that did not permit life: the deep and the darkness. Bringing them forth into a loving creation called good, the Creator didn't destroy those elements, but made them a part of life's rhythm. The path of love begins in Creation and culminates when the stone rolls away at the break of Easter morning.

Using This Book

Whether you use this book alone, with a spouse or friend, or in a group, try to set a pattern that will be intentional and helpful. Here is one pattern that I have found useful:

Each week:
- Before the walk, read the weekly Scripture and reflection. (If you are walking with others, the group may choose to read these before gathering.)
- Read Questions for the Walk. These are purposely open-ended, to encourage thought and discussion during the walk.
- Begin your walk. If you are with a group, expect people to fan out along the path.
- As you walk, consider the Scripture, reflection, and questions; and discuss them if you are with others.

- Gather a half-mile before the end of the walk. Listen to the Scripture again.
- Walk the rest of the way in silence.
- At the end of the walk, offer the closing prayer or a prayer of your own.

Each day:
- Read the daily Scripture and meditation.
- Walk if you can.

Walking Bible Study

I have been walking in circles in the woods
of Tennessee for most of my life. This year
I am trying to walk a circle in the woods every
day. I am feeling grateful for every step—rain,
sleet, or shine—and am aware that this is one
of the ways I can pray and commune
with God.

This Bible study is an invitation to walk
more often, with a renewed sense of spiritual
grounding and kinship. It is a call to individuals, couples, friends, and church groups to
leave living rooms and Sunday school classes
and go outside—to the woods, to a park, to
a bench beneath a tree. It is a mindful practice,
like prayer or service.

While we walk, we are leaving no carbon
footprint; we are not eating, drinking, e-mail-
ing, sleeping, or waiting. We are just walking.
Our goal in this study is not to over-think the
Scriptures, not to dress them up for others to

marvel at, but to let them strip us down, to let them form us and sink in like our footprints in the dirt.

Walking in nature is not an afterthought of spiritual development and practice; it is central, historical, and essential. Contemplating the creator of the universe while walking in God's creation opens our hearts and minds to the wondrous gift of life. This walking Bible study can be a kind of field guide, a tool to learn more about Scripture as we travel through the woods and through our lives.

The insights gained while walking will add to the depth and joy of Bible study. A walking Bible study allows us to study Scripture while practicing a spiritual discipline and may provide the permission some need to move from a classroom onto more solid sacred ground. It may be the only way some individuals will feel comfortable opening themselves to Scripture.

Walking is a gentle, neutral activity; it is not intended to stress our bodies, but to focus our energies while our minds wander and empty. Walking can provide the solution to many of life's problems; it is how we make molehills out of mountains. It is how we wander in the desert, find our way on retreat, make our way to altars and through labyrinths.

To those who are not able to walk or who struggle to do it, I want to say that some of my best walks in the woods have included babies in backpacks; friends in wheelchairs; my husband on a cane, able to go just a short distance before the arthritis took hold of him. Accommodating someone who is slow can be a gift; that person is usually miles ahead in other ways.

Trust that the walk is what it needs to be, and trust your fellow walkers. Read the signs offered in front of you, and mark them. Lay aside any worries that are too heavy to carry into the woods, and remember that you can always pick them up when you leave. Carry the minimum: maybe water, pen, paper, a book, a key. You don't need a pack.

Walk—rain or shine, winter or summer—and don't worry.

Walking in Circles

There is something special about walking in a circle. It is a simple demonstration of the truth that life is a journey, not a destination. It mirrors the world in orbit around the sun and the moon around us. A circle is a symbol of all that is eternal. Our journey begins with God and ends with God; life comes full circle into that truth.

There is a vast difference between walking in a circle and going to a destination. If we have a fixed goal, we can move only in one direction; but our faith journey takes all of us on circuitous routes, sometimes back to the beginning, sometimes around new bends we never expected.

Walking in circles is a way of placing our bodies and minds before the Lord, as did pilgrims, monks, and ascetics before us. Walking on familiar routes frees us up to discover new details and experience different feelings while we walk.

Walking in all weather and during all seasons is an added joy of walking in circles. For twenty years I have walked circles around Radnor Lake, a state park in Tennessee. On a cold, damp winter morning I can tell you where the larkspur, trout lily, and Dutchmen's breeches will bloom come spring. I have felt spiritual renewal like baptism in fresh spring rains. I have felt purified by the cleansing that happens on an August walk at noon, after the sweat, like salty tears, washes away the pain. I have felt awe on a fall afternoon beneath a canopy of leaves that spreads overhead like the ceiling of a cathedral. All these things happen on the same path as I walk the circle again.

Why We Walk

Walking changes us; it can transport our spirits from being weighed down by life into the joy of God's presence. It can clarify epiphanies, offer us grace, remind us of our need for repentance, and hold us accountable to our brothers and sisters.

Walking is a gift. To go on a spiritual journey
without nature as a primary teacher seems like
a Eucharist without bread; we miss out on
something both symbolic and substantive.
Abraham, Buddha, Mohammed, and Jesus all
spent defining parts of their ministry in the
woods gaining inspiration, insight, rest, and
renewal. The woods are our inheritance
and offer us a gift. They provide an area for
learning and humble us before the creator
of the universe.

I have several hopes for this Bible study.
I hope that the context in which we study and
reflect on the Scriptures will provide new
insights into their depth and meaning. I hope
that as we become more familiar with the text,
we will find the freedom to claim new insights
for ourselves, without fear of reprisal or rejec-
tion. Finally, I hope that we use this living
word to influence the way we walk as we leave
the woods and encounter fellow pilgrims in
all the places we walk in our lives.

Pear Blossoms for Sadie

I saw her walk toward the barn
With baby Sadie in tow
As pear blossoms fell like snow
On the christening gown.
Petals like unceasing prayers fell on Sadie
Whose mother just a few winters back
Walked this same field as snow fell
And sealed love upon her heart.
Snow and pear blossoms in fields
Are almost too much to bear
As love rains down upon us
And covers us with blessings.

Week 1. The Creator's Vision

Genesis 1:1-4, 11-13, 20, 24-25, 31

Reflection

The story of our faith begins with the Creation narratives, in which the act of Creation itself becomes the unfolding of God's love for the whole world.

God's love is written all over creation. It begins when God takes the deep and the darkness and, instead of destroying these things, makes them part of creation. God calls it very good. To me, this means that nature is good, we are good, and we are all created together by a loving God who destroys nothing in creating—deep and darkness, earth and light, knit together in a creation that is both unified and diverse.

In this story, creation comes effortlessly from the spoken word of God; and Eden springs from a dream of what is good and lovely. Nature is sacred; it was made by the same creator who made us. If we want to love, worship, and be with God, then it makes sense for us to stand in the midst of creation. The closer we are to nature, the nearer we must be to the heart and desire of the Creator. God is the source of creation.

Recently I took a long walk on the coast of Ecuador. I wandered down a dusty road in a small town at noontime. The town was empty. I thought maybe the residents were out gathering their fishing nets or working in the fields.

I saw a church, and on the cross atop its steeple were perched two huge buzzards. I wanted to look inside the church, but the front doors were padlocked with thick chains. The glassless windows had vertical wrought-iron bars; and I peered between them into the gray, unlit chancel. The sanctuary was completely abandoned. The only one left in the church was Jesus, hanging life-size on a dusty cross above the altar. It looked as if he had been hanging in that same spot for a hundred years.

Between the buzzards, the locked doors, and the dusty crucifix, the church looked like death incarnate. It scared me. It called to mind all the places in the world and in my heart that seemed forsaken. I wondered if maybe our creator had finally had enough and had abandoned creation. I got a terrible sinking feeling, and it made me want to run or cry. What if love won't have the last word? What if creation fails?

I thought about walking away but didn't want to give up. So I looked through the barred windows again, this time with conviction instead of fear. And I saw something else in that old church. Hanging across the front of the church was a row of small, square cloths that children had painted with suns, trees, and butterflies. It looked like a rainbow of prayers carrying the deepest desires of their hearts to a living and loving God. How could I not have seen that before? There was a vase of flowers set in front of the Blessed Sacrament, a sign of living bread. There was a dove's nest in the rafter between the tin roof and the concrete wall. Creation was still giving life to the church and its people, and love was still there.

On the path of love, it is not so much what we look at that is important, but what we see. There is no place on God's green earth where we can look and not see love. That is why, when we finally make the earth our bed, we can rest easy. Love always has the last word. It is the fabric of the earth.

The gift of creation comes to us in a million different ways, and it will take a lifetime of walking in that creation to absorb even a part of it. The gift is in every animal of every kind. It is in every bird of every kind. It is in every plant of every kind. Everything in the Creation story was a part of God's unfolding act of love.

Our job in walking the path of love is to keep looking with new eyes, over and over and over again, trying to take in the manifold gifts before us. They are unbelievable gifts; and it is a joy to celebrate, protect, and honor them.

Questions for the Walk

1. Where do you see evidence of God's loving
   Spirit in nature? Where do you see evidence
   to the contrary? How do you reconcile these
   very different elements?

2. Can you see yourself as a reflection of the
   image of God? Can you see others? What
   does it mean to be a reflection of God's
   image? How does it make you feel?

3. Describe a place or experience that made
   you feel that God had forsaken the world.
   What are your thoughts and feelings about
   it today?

Walk in Silence

Closing Prayer

O Heavenly Creator, who has filled the world with love, open our eyes to behold your gracious hand in all your works, that rejoicing in your whole creation, we may learn to serve you with gladness for the sake of your love that created all things. Teach us the path of love where walking closer to you is our desire and serving others is our joy. Amen.

Meditations for Week

Day 1
In our prayers for you we always thank Go
the Father of our Lord Jesus Christ, for we
have heard of your faith in Christ Jesus and
of the love that you have for all the saints.
                              (Colossians 1:3-4)

I sat in the back of a dimly lit cathedral.
Outside, the bright spring day was in full
bloom. Inside, the lights were low; and a row
of flickering candles on the altar pointed
toward a sacred and shadowed space.

There were about fifty priests in front of
me, mostly with gray haloed hair, bent forward in prayer. What struck me, beyond the
sea of black shirts draped with old sweaters,
was how all their backs looked a little
stooped. I imagined the years of prayers they
had said and the thousands of miles they had
walked, trying to sow love in their part of the

hat journey was almost

ousands of trips to
ind to cemeteries for
at all the prayers they
loated in the air around me,
ed in the heart of God. I thought
at the years of listening and bearing the
burdens of those who had suffered and reached
out for help. There was something beautiful
about the suffering they seemed to be carrying
in their bodies, and I wanted to believe that it
was worth it all.

Then we said amen, and I headed back into
the bright sun to continue my own pilgrim's
walk.

Day 2
As I looked, a stormy wind came out of the
north: a great cloud with brightness around
it and fire flashing forth continually, and in
the middle of the fire, something like gleam-
ing amber. (Ezekiel 1:4)

Ezekiel has wild visions, presents vivid imagery, and preaches dramatic sermons. He sets it all in a rich, natural world that is a powerful teacher.

A deep and complex man, Ezekiel preached from around 593 to 571 BC during hard times to a suffering people about a rich God. He begins with doom and ends with consolation, reminding all of us about the importance of hope, even when we feel exiled or hopeless. In the midst of his visions he sees something gleaming, something beautiful and promising in the midst of something frightening.

I walked with a woman who was recovering from a brain aneurism. She walked every step of the path carefully and slowly, and she talked about nothing but love meeting her at every turn. She revealed the gleaming amber she had found in the prayers and presence of her friends and caregivers in the midst of her storm. While much of the previous month seemed to her like a hazy vision, she could feel deep love imbuing the days with light. While she was telling her story, she would stop and remark about how beautiful a tree or plant was that with normal vision would seem unremarkable. She was a prophet, reminding me to see love in stormy skies and hope in the midst of troubled times.

Ezekiel told us always to trust God, even as we face new challenges. Ironically, it is believed that Ezekiel himself was exiled as he was writing his final words about God's undying care for us.

Day 3
Keep your heart with all vigilance,
  for from it flow the springs of life. . . .
Let your eyes look directly forward,
  and your gaze be straight before you.
Keep straight the path of your feet,
  and all your ways will be sure.
                          (Proverbs 4:23, 25-26)

If we want to guard our hearts, the source of the springs of our lives, we'd better head to the hills.

John Muir, one of the great lovers of the woods and a protector of wild lands, urged us fifty years ago to climb the mountains and get their good tidings. He told us that the winds blow their freshness into us, renewing the well-springs in our hearts. In the hills, all our cares will drop off like autumn leaves.

To refresh our hearts and keep them healthy and loving, we need to walk to the mountains. We can get there on just a whispered prayer offered for the sake of love. To go to the mountains is one of the lessons of every prophet, teacher, and sage. It is where we can keep our hearts strong, where we can glimpse the possibilities of our lives, where we can find strength to go back into the valley to serve. The lesson for me is simple: No matter what, keep walking toward the mountains.

Just because we go to the mountains, though, it doesn't mean we are out of the woods. We must stay focused on why we are making the journey. If it is not to learn about love, we might as well not make the effort.

Thoreau says that all we have to do is pursue some path, however narrow or crooked, that we can walk with love and reverence. If we can walk with love toward the mountains, all our steps will be sure.

Day 4
Let your light so shine before men, that they may see your good works and glorify your Father in heaven. (Matthew 5:16, NKJV)

I didn't notice the bluebird until she took flight. Her color blended into the branches, and she was small and unremarkable in the midst of the forest scene. But when she spread her iridescent blue wings and darted through the air, my heart flew with her. Three other bluebirds followed, taking flight through the woods that now seemed lovelier for their beautiful presence.

Whenever we are given the grace to take flight on our path, I pray we are that beautiful. I pray we are not ashamed of our beauty or hide it from anyone. Our light, if we let it shine, can be as lovely as the bluebird's wings in flight. That light sparks light in the hearts of others, making the whole world glow. Hiding its beauty means that the world, like the woods before the bluebird took off, will be less remarkable.

All of us have some stunning shade of blue in our hearts that could add to the beauty in this world and light the path of fellow travelers.

Day 5
Love is patient; love is kind; love is not envious or boastful or arrogant or rude. It does not insist on its own way; it is not irritable or resentful. (1 Corinthians 13:4-5)

I had a rush of jealousy for my woods the other day. All winter long I have been hiking in my favorite parks around the city. The parks have been relatively quiet and empty, except for the squirrels rustling in dry leaves and the songs from nearby birds. Usually I see only a few people as I meditate in the silent woods, and it is possible to stop and write all alone.

That experience may have lulled me into the false notion that somehow these woods are partial to me; that, while I don't own them, we love each other and belong together. These are the woods where I passed the winter contemplating the prophets and dreaming about my faith. These are the woods that I came to appreciate as a fragile treasure to protect and as a strong friend to hold my grief and secrets.

But last week spring came, the hillsides burst into purple majesty, and the people came in droves. There was nowhere to park, and rangers put out traffic cones. I felt protective and jealous of my woods, and then I felt embarrassed that the thought had even crossed my mind.

I know these are not my woods, even if I love them. I know that all the woods and all the land, no matter how well we tend them, build on them, and know them, are never really ours. I love these woods; and so I will walk among their admirers today with no jealousy, just an open heart.

Day 6
Let the little children come to me; do not
stop them; for it is to such as these that the
kingdom of God belongs. (Mark 10:14)

Valerie and I arrived at the beach in South
Carolina. The sunset was already a memory
when she asked if I wanted to go walking
with her.

The beach was dark because the nesting tur-
tles require that no one on that stretch of the
coast turns on houselights that would illumi-
nate the sand. The waxing moon, with Saturn
hanging close, provided all our light. We
walked across a wooden bridge, over the sweet
grass and sea oats out onto the beach. When
we reached the end of the path, Valerie sat
down at the end of the walkway and put her
feet in the sand.

"Will you hold my hand?" she asked.

"OK," I said, "but you don't have to worry.
It's a gentle tide."

"I've never been to the beach and never seen
the ocean," she said. "I'm a little scared."

Valerie is forty-eight years old. She is a graduate of Magdalene, a program for women who have survived lives of addiction, violence, and prostitution. She has seen the inside of prisons, the underside of bridges, and the backside of hands; but she was like a child in front of the ocean's eternal tide. She was afraid of the unknown and wanted a hand.

In today's Scripture, Jesus tells the disciples that we must be like a child to enter the kingdom of God. We must embrace fear and excitement as we walk through this world in new wonder. We must be so amazed by love that we reach out and hold on to a fellow pilgrim when she is afraid.

Week 2. Moses' Vision

Exodus 33:12, 18-23

Reflection

When we walk in God's creation, we are close to the heart of the Creator. God pronounced the creation very good, and as part of it we are too.

As the story of God's people unfolds in the Bible, the path of love is woven throughout. The path, always part of the natural world, is present in the history of Israel, the journey of Jesus, and the mission of the early church. Over and over again we are reminded that it is our path as well. We are called to walk in faith close to God and to trust that he always has our best interests at heart. At every twist and turn in the story of faith, God is found in the wilderness, in the mountain, in the night, helping us as we stumble along the path of love.

Moses' life and ministry embodied the path of love. Moses' mother began his journey by releasing him into the wild river. She put him in a basket and set him in the hands of the river, trusting that God's loving mercy would keep him safe. Eventually Moses found his way back into the wild to hear God in the burning bush, calling him to liberate his people. After Moses led the people through wild waters, he spent his life wandering in the wild desert, learning the basic law of love that is still imprinted on our hearts from the Book of Deuteronomy: "Hear, O Israel: The LORD is our God, the LORD alone. You shall love the LORD your God with all your heart, and with all your soul, and with all your might" (Deuteronomy 6:4-5).

In this week's Scripture we see Moses heading into the wild again as he makes his way up Mount Sinai for a meeting with God. Mount Sinai was not the Promised Land, but it played a critical role in forming the group of refugees into a nation. Sinai was where the covenant relationship with Israel was formed, the holy mountain where the laws were given.

Moses practiced walking a faithful path of love in his life, journeying deep into the mountains many times. He willingly followed that path through the desert and onto the cliffs. When Moses' desire to see God overcame him, God called him to come up onto the holy mountain.

Mountains play a central role in all spiritual journeys, as real or symbolic places where our hearts are led to be with God. The path of love likewise is a place where the heart leads, though sometimes it is only later that our heads follow. In the mountains, the air is thinner and sometimes makes our heads spin.

Last year, I ascended the steepest hill I had ever climbed. I can't say that God called me to the hill; it felt like the hill itself called me. It made my heart race just to look at the trail. It was made up of acute angles of rocky terrain stretching toward the sky. There were jagged black boulders beneath the cliffs that would provide little break for a fall.

When I started up the hill, I found that I could barely climb without using my hands; and I kept wondering how in the world

I would get down. It gripped my heart as sweat seeped from every pore, stinging my eyes. But I promise it was worth it.

Once I was on top, there was nothing but wild weeds that blossomed, forgotten by the world below. There were young thistles and passion flowers spread out like a picnic blanket on a spring day. From my high perch I gazed down at raptors that floated upward, drifting toward heaven, on currents only they could feel.

On top of the steepest hill I had ever climbed, I imagined how Moses hid in a rock crevice and saw the back of God's head. I imagined that love was glowing from a bush and calling me to take off my shoes.

Later, I found that going down the hill was just as hard as climbing it. It seemed impossible that I wouldn't fall, so I braced myself for the worst. Descending from the vistas and the sweet, breezy air onto solid ground made my mouth dry. Finally, back on even ground, I was left dreaming that someday I might once again ascend the steepest hill I had ever climbed.

I love the idea that Moses wanted to see God,

not just hear his words or follow his commandments. So God, who loved Moses, said that the closest he would come to seeing the Creator was to stand on a rock and hide his face.

This was a sign of reconciliation between God and the people. After the Israelites broke their covenant with God while in the desert, Moses learned that he would be given a sign of the loving bond between God and God's people. God told him, "While my glory passes by I will put you in a cleft of the rock, and I will cover you with my hand until I have passed by; then I will take away my hand, and you shall see my back; but my face shall not be seen" (Exodus 33:22-23).

Imagine the back of God's head. No one has seen the face of God; but in the mountains we, like the founding fathers of Christianity, Judaism, and Islam, can glimpse a part of him. It is reassuring to me that the beloved servant of God, who followed God into the wilderness and died there before he ever saw the Promised Land, only glimpsed the back of God's head. It means that the loving relationship between creator and creation remains a mystery and a longing.

No one can fully take in the glory of the Lord and live. All we can do is keep walking a path of love through the desert and into the holy mountains.

Questions for the Walk

1. How does it make you feel to think that you, as part of the creation, were pronounced by God to be very good?

2. Why do you think many of the prophets' revelations and conversations with God happened in the wilderness?

3. Our paths don't always feel like paths of love. What does your path feel like today?

4. Have you ever taken on a physical challenge that scared you? If so, what was the challenge? What happened? What did you learn?

Walk in Silence

Closing Prayer

Gracious and loving God, in your compassion you call us on our paths to draw near to you. Open our eyes and ears and hearts in the wilderness to hear that call again. You go before us and behind us; you are our light on the wilderness path. Be our clear sight, and keep us close to your heart all the days of our lives. Amen.

Meditations for Week 2

Day 1
And you shall be like a watered garden,
  like a spring of water,
    whose waters never fail. (Isaiah 58:11b)

I have never thought that squirrels were
much to look at, but the other day I fell in love
with one.

I was walking along one evening when
a squirrel scampered out onto a limb. The
setting sun hit the squirrel in such a way
that he was in a pure, haloed light. He
glowed from his head to his bushy tail. Suddenly I saw the squirrel as one of the most
beautiful creations in the world, and the
woods lit up.

Sometimes this world seems almost too beautiful to bear; it is so rich and diverse that we are
not able to comprehend it. When those
moments fill my heart, I feel like a part of

Isaiah's vision of the Kingdom coming. I feel like
a spring of water that overflows in gratitude.

It is a gift to discover that we are part
of a vision of love so powerful that our well of
gratitude will never dry up. We are part of God's
garden, as beautiful as the squirrel at sunset.

Day 2
  I have loved you with an everlasting love;
  I have drawn you with loving-kindness. . . .

  Again you will take up your tambourines
  and go out to dance with the joyful.

Again you will plant vineyards
  on the hills of Samaria;
  the farmers will plant them
  and enjoy their fruit.
                        (Jeremiah 31:3-5, NIV)

There was never a time when God did not
love us. Even in the hard truth-telling of the
prophet Jeremiah, God never stops loving
us. Even as Jeremiah prophesies about the

worst of the path, the part where we are afraid
and exiled, he never doubts God's love. He
speaks as one who knows the depths of despair,
has witnessed the destruction of his home, and
still believes that God's love for us is greater.
Jeremiah keeps preaching and teaching, never
thinking that he has arrived, but rather realiz-
ing there is always more to do for the sake
of love.

Throughout his life Jeremiah possessed
a profound sensitivity to God's love. Even
though he ended up dying exiled in Egypt, Jeremiah calls us to walk faithfully, always seeing
the work ahead as a gift to love more deeply. He
never doubted that, because of God's profound
love for his people, we will someday take up
tambourines and dance for joy.

Jeremiah's words remind me of Anne
Frank, who, in her own despair and exile in
an isolated space with no hope of walking
outside, wrote that the best remedy "for
those who are afraid, lonely or unhappy is to
go outside, somewhere where they can be
quiet, alone with the heavens, nature and

God. Because only then does one feel that all is as it should be."

Anne Frank died of typhoid in a labor camp at the age of fifteen, a few weeks before liberation, never able to take the walk she had envisioned. Jeremiah also died in exile. If Anne Frank and Jeremiah could see the walk as a path to a loving God, surely we can too.

Day 3
He covers the sky with clouds;
he supplies the earth with rain
and makes grass grow on the hills.
                              (Psalm 147:8, NIV)

Loving parents supply all their children's most basic needs without the need for praise. It is just what parents do, because they love their children. God does too.

The other day, because I didn't have much time, I took my walk through the neighborhood. It always feels like a compromise to walk around the city streets and miss out on the parks, where there are no cars or cell phone coverage.

As I walked, I decided the problem was that the neighborhood feels mundane to me. It is a little boring to walk there. I feel as if I have done it a million times. I have seen the potholes in the street and the curve to the left as the road rises. I know how long it takes for the light to change and which dogs to avoid.

The truth is that I have taken these old neighborhood streets for granted. I haven't been giving thanks for grass and water and planted annual flowers. I haven't marveled at the hackberries in most of the yards or celebrated the sky that peeks out between the buildings and telephone wires. Because I have taken all this for granted, my life is poorer.

The psalmist, who doesn't take God for granted, created one of the most beautiful psalms of praise in honor of God's sweet love. It is a gift to remember that rain and grass are signs of God's loving care for us and creation.

Day 4
I led them with cords of human kindness,
* with bands of love.*
I was to them like those
* who lift infants to their cheeks.*
I bent down to them and fed them.
(Hosea 11:4)

I walked through Audubon Park in New Orleans. The park is over a hundred years old, with alleys of ancient water oaks. As you pass between the oaks, you realize that they carry the memory of the Civil War in their twisted limbs and bark. Along the promenade, the oaks are decked out in long gray moss and beautiful resurrection ferns that grow the length of their branches.

In one stretch, there is a pond with a rookery of ibis a thousandfold. These migrating birds have made the old oaks their winter home before heading back north on their journey. The ibis light on the fern-draped branches and make nests from the moss at the junction of the trunk and limbs. The males fluff their long tail feathers and dance for mates in a vision that would fill Hosea with joy.

This harmony of the passing seasons, with dancing birds on steady limbs, reminds us of the bonds of love. You can imagine that the long oak limbs dipping toward the earth are literally bending to offer respite to the ibis travelers. The ibis, seemingly forgetting that this is just a temporary home, fall in love and dance; and out of it new life emerges that will continue this pattern for another hundred years. The beauty of the sight stops me in my tracks. I try to hold on to the image and keep it from slipping through the cracks of time.

Love will always tie us to each other and to the earth, as long as we walk in love and are willing to bend down to feed one another.

Day 5
May God grant me to speak with judgment,
   and to have thoughts worthy of what I
      have received;

for he is the guide even of wisdom
    and the corrector of the wise.
        (Wisdom of Solomon 7:15, Apocrypha)

I was walking down a quiet road, not thinking about anything in particular—at least,
I have no memory of what I was thinking
about when a thought came to me. It arrived
while I wasn't looking and blindsided me. It
seemed to come from nowhere and fill me with
a brand-new idea. It woke me up to myself.

I could feel my heart beating and my feet
inside my shoes hitting the road. I changed my
pace so I would be quieter and not scare the
thought away. I still was not sure where it had
come from or exactly where it would lead me.
I did hope it would stay a while, because it was
great company. The thought stirred other
thoughts that must have been resting in my
head. It gave me a feeling of being in love with
the moment. It provided sweet communion
between a solitary person and the thoughts that
spring up on a cloudless day, just walking
down the road.

Soon the thought became just the memory of a thought, and I wondered if someone else had thought it first and then sent it my way. Was it born in the wind? Did the sunlight conspire with a leaf to move in such a way that I could grasp it? I think my thought knew my prayers and had come as an unexpected answer. I hope it goes on to new places and meets people who never dreamed of thinking the thought. I hope other new thoughts come my way again out of the blue. Those are the sweet thoughts that gently move us from sleepwalking to an awakening of love in the blink of an eye.

Day 6
Come, my beloved,
  let us go forth into the fields,
  and lodge in the villages;
let us go out early to the vineyards,
  and see whether the vines have budded,
whether the grape blossoms have opened
  and the pomegranates are in bloom.
                    (Song of Solomon 7:11-12)

Love calls us to go out to the fields and woods. It pulls us to celebrate something bigger than us in a space that is large enough to contain the joy and mystery of love.

If you have walked through the whole winter, there is nothing like walking with someone you love to see the first buds of spring. If you have walked through the depth of your sadness, there is nothing like seeing the daffodils begin to open up, signaling that all of life is getting ready to blossom. The new life of spring calls us to fall in love, not just with another person, but with the blossoming creation itself. Creation calls us to come, see its beauty, and celebrate the love that permeates it all.

The Song of Songs was written as part of a collection of songs that, together in the Hebrew Scripture, was called the greatest song. The collection praises the depth of love and includes yearning, admiration, and reminiscing about love. It refers to the depth and breadth of love that God holds for his people.

In this passage, the man has already declared his great passion for the woman. Now the woman invites him to the fields to be together and witness the reawakening of nature.

Week 3. Mark's Vision

Mark 10:28-31

Reflection

We have seen how the path of love moves from the Creation narrative that grounds our walk in love into the story of Moses that renews a loving relationship with God. This week, through Mark, we witness a beautiful lesson by Jesus as he tells the disciples how to follow the path of love.

The gospel story itself shows the path of love that is traveled by our Lord. It is the path the disciples are trying to follow during the years when they are "on their way" to Jerusalem. In the Gospel of Mark, the lessons and parables that explain the way to walk this path as disciples come in quick vignettes and sayings by Jesus.

When Jesus sent the Twelve on their healing ministry, he "ordered them to take nothing for their journey except a staff; no bread, no bag, no money in their belts; but to wear sandals and not to put on two tunics. He said to them, 'Wherever you enter a house, stay there until you leave the place. If any place will not welcome you and they refuse to hear you, as you leave, shake off the dust that is on your feet.' " (Mark 6:8-11).

Jesus has just described what may be the first liturgical dance. When we do not find peace on our path, we shake the dust off our feet so nothing sticks to us; and we continue on our way with no bitterness or fear. Shaking off the dust enables us to discard the past like baggage so that we can walk freely.

In the eighth chapter of Mark, after Jesus has spent time preaching and healing throughout Judah, he reminds his followers that those who want to walk this path must lose their life for the sake of the gospel (Mark 8:35). The demanding path requires of us that we live for love, taking up our crosses and walking in faith.

In the Gospels, Jesus teaches us what the ideal path of love looks like. To me, the lesson is that it is not an easy road, although the gifts along the way make us unbelievably grateful. Sometimes it seems impossible to carry out what love demands, including loving our enemies, giving up our family ties, and getting rid of anything that stands between us and the fulfillment of the mission.

Our Lord tells us that we can't be comfortable on the path; we need to keep searching for a better way to live. It means we will live like foxes that never find holes and birds that don't settle in nests. We will be in the wilderness, searching for a place to lay down our hearts for the sake of love. It is truly a path toward home, always remembering we are not home yet. We are wanderers in the world, called to love it and be a part of its healing.

Preceding this week's reading, Jesus has fed five thousand and then four thousand hungry people, has walked up the mountain to visit God, and is telling us again about love's way. The passage is about the consequences of

choosing the path of discipleship. In the verses
leading up to it, Jesus has spoken to a rich man
about entering heaven with his possessions,
saying it would be easier for a camel to pass
through the eye of a needle.

When the passage begins, Peter reminds
Jesus that their path has cost them everything.
In context, it seems as if Peter is saying that the
disciples are poor because of their desire to follow Jesus. Jesus acknowledges that there has
been a cost in surrendering to love, but he
points out that on the path not everything lines
up the way we think it should. There is value in
walking at the back of the line; and since there
are riches in what the world deems to be poor,
we can't always see what is of eternal worth.
We can't walk like a Pharisee, wanting always
to win, or like the rich man, wanting to
keep everything.

The path of love requires us to be vulnerable,
to be in need of others' mercy, and to be willing
to lose for love's sake. As long as we are serving and trying to love our neighbors, the walk
continues. Our faith grows and changes as it

encounters the world. We let things go and are willing to lose in order to gain the lessons of love. We seek out the wilderness of the world where we have never walked before. In walking, we learn what discipleship means.

I will never forget the time I walked in the Kalahari Desert. I was there because I had decided not to show up for my job at a local church in Gaborone, Botswana. My feelings had been hurt by their position on the ordination of women; and one morning I just decided that instead of working, I would head out with a friend into the desert.

My friend was a young Botswana woman; and through a combination of bad luck and funny coincidence, we ended up stranded about eighty miles into the desert. We had an entire afternoon to sit under a tree and think about everything that had taken us there and ponder how grateful we would be if some kind soul would happen by and take mercy on us.

Just as the sun began to turn orange and hang near the horizon, a nomadic bush group appeared. They took us in, fed us with no questions or judgment, and gave us animal skins sewn together for bedding. The next day a medical truck gave us a ride to a town close to Namibia.

The experience all those years ago has left me filled with gratitude and amazed at how love finds us on the road. When I was the most lost I have ever been, love was just around the bend, ready to meet me.

Questions for the Walk

1. Listen to the sound of your own footsteps. What do you hear? How are your footsteps different from others? What do those differences reveal about you?

2. If you were going to shake dust off your feet, what dust would it be? Where did it come from?

3. Where would you go instead?

4. How do you feel about the prospect of never growing comfortable in your journey of faith? In your life now, what are the areas of comfort and discomfort?

5. What is the most lost that you have ever been? How did you respond? What, if anything, did you learn from the experience?

Walk in Silence

Closing Prayer
(Attributed to Francis of Assisi)

Lord, make us instruments of your peace.
Where there is hatred, let us sow love; where
there is injury, pardon; where there is discord,
union; where there is doubt, faith; where there
is despair, hope; where there is darkness, light;
where there is sadness, joy. Grant that we may
not so much seek to be consoled as to console;
to be understood, as to understand; to be
loved, as to love. For it is in giving that we
receive; it is in pardoning that we are par-
doned; and it is in dying that we are born to
eternal life. Amen.

Meditations for Week 3

Day 1
Make a joyful noise to the LORD,
all the earth.
Worship the LORD *with gladness;*
come into his presence with singing.
(Psalm 100:1-2)

A battalion of geese honked revelry on the
lake today.

Every year their procession across the water
signals the annual pilgrimage south. The flight
formations look like a magic trick, until they
land with flapping wings and honking
voices. They are as loud as a Baptist revival or
a family reunion with tons of aunts. It sounds
as though they haven't seen each other in years
and have a million stories to share. I imagine
them going fishing later and getting reac-
quainted. I have read that they mate for life, so
I try to pair up who goes with whom.

After the geese pass by the lake and head into the hills, their honking transforms into a song in praise of creation as it echoes round the bend. They become a choir of love, singing the first hymn ever written. Since they are birds, they have been around as long as dinosaurs; so there is a chance they wrote one of the first songs ever heard.

Someday I want to join this joyful noise. I want to gather with a community and lift our collective voice without a thought about how it looks or sounds to another person. We will just throw back our heads and open our lungs to sing a big alleluia to the Creator and this amazing creation.

Day 2
Now the whole group of those who believed were of one heart and soul. (Acts 4:32)

It is so beautiful when things come together. It is a gift when what we are trying to achieve and what others want to achieve arrive in harmony, so we can live for a moment with one heart and soul.

It can happen on a walk, when a group gathers and the Spirit is there with everyone being open to each other. There is a groove you can fall into, where even during crisis there is a sweet spot on the path. I love the very idea of a sweet spot. In baseball, the pitch crosses the plate right in the strike zone where you can hit it. In playing a guitar, you find the perfect space between the bridge and frets where the music rings out with beautiful, harmonic tones. In nature, the sweet spot is the color of bluebonnets, located somewhere between purple and blue.

On the spiritual path there are many sweet spots: where you achieve clarity and feel a wave of compassion for victims of injustice, where your heart is emptied and freedom rushes in, where defiance meets surrender and you want to wash your neighbor's feet as an act of faith, where humility meets courage and you feel ready to face your fears with new energy, where life meets death and old lines that have been drawn in the sand blow away with the slightest breeze.

The act of walking allows sweet spots to grow. It takes you to a place where the hard lessons of the gospel meet daily acts of loving without judgment, and all of us move along the path with one heart and soul.

Day 3
Let not the sun go down upon your wrath.
(Ephesians 4:26, KJV)

When I saw the sun set over the ocean, the experience was so powerful that it took up permanent residence in my memory.

I don't know how there could have been a thousand sunsets, and then one day a particular sunset leaped out and set me on the right course again. The sun blushed, turning from yellow to orange to a glowing pink coral as she kissed the day goodbye. Maybe she was surprised by her own power and beauty that cause the world to stop and turn her way, write poetry, sail into her arms.

I was in love with that sunset and with all the metaphors of her life. For a moment she emptied me of any trace of doubt or fear of tomorrow. Eternity was in her sights and for-giveness in her shadow. She made it easy for me to fulfill Paul's advice to the Ephesians—not by any effort on my part, but because of her great warmth and the healing power of her love.

I know what it is like to feel anger in the heat of the day. Paul's letter offers a way out of that anger and a return to the path of love. All we have to do is turn to the sunset on our next walk and watch wrath's bitterness melt as the evening sun washes over it. Her beauty can be a healing balm.

Day 4
The earth is full of the goodness of the
    LORD. *(Psalm 33:5, KJV)*

I was hiking on the hem of America in the hills of the Olympic Peninsula, off the shore of Washington. I could see intricate vertical hills that looked like folds on a shirt tucked gracefully into a dark, silky, watery skirt. I felt as if I were part of a beautifully braided border sewn at the continent's edge.

Above the trail, an eagle soared and Indian paintbrush wildflowers pushed through snow-capped hills. The whole world was filled with the goodness of the Lord, and I felt myself move into deep worship.

Ralph Waldo Emerson says that we should never miss an opportunity to see anything beautiful in nature: "It is God's handwriting— a wayside sacrament. Welcome it in every fair face, every fair sky, and every fair flower." The earth is filled with the goodness of the Lord, the psalmist sings. Because it is filled with goodness, it overflows into our hearts and minds as we walk. It settles our souls, and problems that seemed important simply fade away in the wilderness.

Sometimes it's hard to believe that we can just walk on God's green earth. It seems too beautiful to be true. At times like these, we see that nature is God's handwriting; and it is full of goodness.

Day 5
Jesus, full of the Holy Spirit, returned from
the Jordan and was led by the Spirit in the
wilderness. (Luke 4:1)

It seems reasonable to me that the Spirit
would lead our Lord into the wilderness. When
the person in the wilderness is I, it's harder
to imagine.

I don't mind the wilderness if I have a map,
phone, guide, and guarantee that none of the
snakes are poisonous. Otherwise, even if
I believe I am walking in the presence of love,
the idea of wilderness is frightening.

A pastor I know is experiencing a hard
patch of road lately—really hard. She
describes how, in the wilderness where she
finds herself, she caught a glimpse of love
around an unexpected turn. In the midst of
being lost, grieving, and searching, she dis-
covered an exquisite tenderness and felt
found by a loving God.

Jesus headed to the wilderness with everything he needed to make it through. He took

the knowledge of his faith tradition as a guide to use when tempted to leave the path, and he carried love that led him deeper into the truth.

All of us carry everything we need to make it through the wilderness. We carry a history, spirit, and love. We don't simply waltz through, thank God. Instead we venture out, knowing that we are dust and to dust we shall return. We go alone, driven to search our hearts and our world all over again.

When we go to the wilderness, we catch a glimpse of love's power to heal, restore, and find us around some unexpected turn. The wilderness may scare us, but it is a gift on this journey of love.

Day 6
But Thomas (who was called the Twin), one of the twelve, was not with them when Jesus came. So the other disciples told him, "We have seen the Lord." But he said to them, "Unless I see the mark of the nails in his hands, and put my finger in the mark of the

nails and my hand in his side, I will not believe." (John 20:24-25)

There are mornings when I don't want to talk, and a million excuses start creeping in. I also have mornings when doubt wakes me up and escorts me around as though I am blind. It is those mornings when more than ever I need to walk. I need to believe that as soon as my foot hits the trail, the confusion and laziness of my life will subside and I can "come round right," as the old Shaker hymn says.

Doubt is a great teacher. Sometimes it's rooted in feelings of unworthiness, which makes it about us, not about God. Usually before I finish a mile, I can already sense doubt lifting as I feel sympathy for my own shortcomings and com-passion for everyone else's. I am just one hiker on a million miles of trail, spanning millennia, hoping that my weak faith is enough for God.

Doubts and distractions can lead us toward a compassionate faith. When I get up close to my own doubts, they make me a more effective disciple.

I love the apostle Thomas. I want to tell him that his doubts have freed a lot of people and have kept them coming back to the woods. He teaches us that mistakes are the communion of compassion toward humanity. He reminds us of the need for mercy more than justice.

Week 4. Paul's Vision

Romans 12:9-18

Reflection

The witness of the early church reminds us that it is more important how we walk than where we walk.

The path of love is a missionary journey. Wherever we are, if we walk in love, we are bearing witness to the love of God in Christ. The goal of the community is to walk generously and peaceably, with freedom that allows love to flourish.

Even with the distractions, obligations, and time constraints that we face today, as a community of faith we can walk together with the simple intention of loving God with our whole heart and our neighbors as ourselves. In Paul's letter to the Romans, he reminds us how important it is to walk with genuine affection for one another; to walk together, rather than to beat each other to the finish line.

It seems to me that the walk is pacifist in nature, seeking love where hate has been. Possibly that is my bias, which I read into most Bible texts. This passage calls us to be present on the walk, to be aware of the world in which we live and to try to make it a better, more loving place. The walk is noble, and it bears witness to the one we follow.

Paul reminds us to be thoughtful and to remember our influence on others; we are teachers as well as students. It is a good and holy journey. We walk with all who have taken the trail before us, those who share the trail with us, and everyone who will follow.

Paul exhorts the church to be a loving community. We must not be hypocrites, talking about our brothers and sisters in disparaging ways and pretending we speak out of love. True love is the central and necessary ingredient for a path of faith. If we walk that path, we will be carrying the spirit of our Lord on the journey.

I walked near a hill of kudzu in the summer. Nothing can change the landscape of pines and tulip poplars like kudzu. It transforms the sweet hillside, like clouds in a clear sky, into strange shapes that look like dream figures. It is easy to see dinosaurs, castles, and gingerbread men.

On this particular walk I saw a crucifix and all the saints, as if I was in the presence of Peter, Paul, and the founders of the faith I am trying to follow. Instead of thinking about them as figures in history, I imagined them watching me from the kudzu. That day nature offered me a way to cut through the eons and continents and to be present with the world's essential truths.

The prophets and teachers of the faith are walking with us; their spirits lead us toward love.

Questions for the Walk

1. "The path of love is a missionary journey." What do you think this statement means?

Do you agree? What examples can you cite from your own life?

2. Can you think of times when you tried to beat others to the finish line? If so, what was the result? Are there times when winning is good?

3. Can you remember a person who taught you how to walk with nobility? What do you remember about that person? How did it affect you?

4. Who are some founders of the faith whom you would walk with? Imagine a conversation with them. What would they tell you? How would you respond?

Walk in Silence

Closing Prayer

Teach us to love our walk, to give thanks for
each step, and to have compassion for all those
who walk beside us. Help us remember all
those who taught us how to walk. Give us the
wisdom and will to teach others how to
walk. You always raise up laborers for your
harvest, to sow and reap love; let us be sowers
of nobility, walking with one heart and mind,
so that love can flourish in this world. Amen.

Meditations for Week 4

Day 1
*This was the appearance of the likeness of
the glory of the LORD. When I saw it, I fell
on my face. (Ezekiel 1:28)*

Once in a blue moon, we get such a stunning
glimpse of God's love that it is almost too
much to bear.

A blue moon is actually the second full
moon that occurs in a calendar month.
Because our calendar months and the lunar
months don't coincide, extra days accumulate
so that every two or three years there is an
extra full moon.

One time, under a blue moon, I think I saw
something like what Ezekiel described. I was
walking in the moonlight on a ridge, and the
roaring wind bent and bowed the tree
limbs. The huge moon danced, and the tree
branches shone. The smile across my chapped

face stuck, and I couldn't speak. All I could do was sit down and marvel at the scene.

If what I saw was anything like Ezekiel's vision, then maybe I came as close as I will ever come to seeing God. In that moment the whole world was filled with glory, and worship seemed as natural as breathing.

Day 2
But those who hope in the L\ord
will renew their strength.
They will soar on wings like eagles;
they will run and not grow weary,
they will walk and not be faint.
                    (Isaiah 40:31, NIV)

You can't predict when your heart is going to soar. It comes on suddenly, like a shadow crossing over you on a sunny day from the wing of a hawk. Looking up, you realize that if the sun and hawk had not lined up in exactly the right way, you never would have seen the hawk in its flight.

The prophets' visions often start out as ordinary scenes; then the light shifts in just the right way, and spirits soar like distant eagles. The moment that sent their heart soaring is then written into the history of faith. It calls us to see all the fleeting gifts we receive as signs of God's lasting love.

Maybe today the wind will blow just right, and someone on the path will turn at that exact instant to catch the wind, and their spirit will soar to the heavens. Moments like that can change the world.

Our hearts are made like eagle's wings; they are created to soar as we walk with loving hearts.

Day 3
For truly I tell you, if you have faith the size of a mustard seed, you will say to this mountain, "Move from here to there," and it will move; and nothing will be impossible for you. (Matthew 17:20)

When walking on the Appalachian Trail, I have been struck by the fact that a very, very long time ago, those mountains weren't there. And they weren't the result of erosion; they were created all at once, when a metamorphic shift occurred and the mountains rose up.

The same thing is possible in faith. There are moments during crises of faith—critical junctures at which something has to give—when love allows faith to send our hearts thrusting toward the sky, making them taller than we could ever have imagined: We face injustice or the suffering of the innocent; we come to terms with our shortcomings and fears; we grieve a beloved friend. At these moments, faith shifts. What we once believed has to change, because we have changed. Faith moves so it can grow.

As we pray, act, study, and live, these changes allow us to love more fully and develop a faith more worthy of our Lord. We learn to forgive ourselves for having a faith that was too small—one that was unwilling to change, that failed to serve a world in pain, that had a history of silencing voices.

Jesus tells us to strengthen our faith. Parables are the tools to till the soil. Forgiveness is the

water to feed it. Our faith will grow like
a mustard seed, and that tiny seed will eventually break through stone hearts. If nourished, it
will allow us to forgive each other for our
shortcomings and to let that forgiveness grow
wild and spread where the wind blows.

Day 4
And suddenly from heaven there came
a sound like the rush of a violent wind, and
it filled the entire house where they were sit-
ting. Divided tongues, as of fire, appeared
among them, and a tongue rested on each of
them. All of them were filled with the Holy
Spirit and began to speak in other languages,
as the Spirit gave them ability. (Acts 2:2-4)

I spent two days at the University of Virginia
listening to Jürgen Moltmann speak to a group
of about twenty pastors. He spoke in a beautiful room with large windows that opened onto
the Jefferson Lawn, which is hedged by azalea
bushes. From a chair facing us with his back to
the window, he spoke about his theology of the
Holy Spirit and the early church.

Moltmann, born in Germany in 1926, is one of the preeminent theologians of our time. His passion is for the realization of the kingdom of God as it exists both in the future and in the present. He said there are two characteristics of the Holy Spirit: first, it comes as a surprise; and second, it is abundant. As he talked about his own life and the Holy Spirit, I could see bright red azaleas through the window. When I squinted, they looked like flames dancing on his head and shoulders.

Sometimes I forget that in my desire to experience the presence of God, I have misunderstood and misused the Holy Spirit. I have treated it as if it were a muse. I act as if the Holy Spirit is present only when we feel it or when we are inspired to act. But the Holy Spirit permeates the world whenever and wherever we walk. It is *Ruach*, the wind spirit; and it moves whether we feel it or not.

I am so thankful to celebrate the gift of the Holy Spirit—that even when we don't know that it's there, we never walk alone. May we see the Holy Spirit as a surprising presence on

all our walks, wild and abundant as azaleas
dancing in the window.

Day 5
You shall love your neighbor as yourself.
                                    (Matthew 22:39)

I could hear the group of women talking
loudly long before I could see them on the
path. Their voices broke through the peaceful
morning in the woods and killed the communion I was sharing with six deer eating nearby.
I was irritated by the women and didn't feel a
bit of love or compassion as they approached.

What was more irritating than the women
was my realization that no matter how much
we practice our spiritual disciplines, feelings of
cynicism, irritation, and anger can crop up
from nowhere and prevent us from loving our
neighbors. When that happens, we build a wall
to separate ourselves from them instead of
inviting them to share the walk.

Everything becomes cloudy when we lose the
clarity and deep truth of this single line from

the Gospels. Our Lord, in this line, renews the mantra that Moses began: Love your neighbor. Don't judge anyone walking by. Don't get angry or offended without reason.

We are called to love the world. How can we do it if we can't even love the stranger who crosses our path today?

Day 6
Then God said, "Let the earth put forth vegetation: plants yielding seed, and fruit trees of every kind on earth that bear fruit with the seed in it." And it was so. The earth brought forth vegetation: plants yielding seed of every kind, and trees of every kind bearing fruit with the seed in it. And God saw that it was good. And there was evening and there was morning, the third day.
(Genesis 1:11-13)

It had been one of the wettest springs I had experienced in years. Garden weddings and outdoor graduations were being held inside sanctuaries and gyms. The rain, falling on soaked soil, pooled and flowed unbounded, filling up streams to overflowing. All of God's abundance was being poured out onto the earth to make an ever-flowing spring. It was like being in the tropics or in Eden itself.

In this vast and rich Eden, the May apple seems best prepared for the moisture. Her single leaf, an umbrella, lets water flow and protects her single blossom. That flower, like all creation, is made in secret, intricately woven in the depths of the earth. It is not fragile or sweet, but miraculous and healing.

As a result, May apples were bigger and more abundant than I had ever seen them. They were strong enough to endure and blossom. The May apple, like love, was made for spring and was flourishing in the wet, wet weather.

This is the creation that God made. We walk in the blessed richness of God's love. We soak in the rain, spread our arms wide, lift our heads, and drink it all in.

I Lay Me Down in Flowers

I lay me down in flowers
The harbingers of spring.
That despite the coming frost
Blossom in unaffected modesty.
They are the spitting image of their past.
The true descendants of grace.
Even though their roots are thin
I can trace them back to Eve's mother.
In fragile spring beauty they swear
They wouldn't miss this day for the world.
The day when hillsides blush in tenderness
And valleys rise in regal style.
I lay me down in flowers just
To feel the blood root petal.
My heart is so full of joy it cannot stand
To think how quickly this will pass.

Notes

Pages 47–48, Frank. See http://thinkexist.com/quota
tion/the_best_remedy_for_those_who_are_afraid
-lonely/144946.html. (5-25-10)

Page 64, Francis of Assisi. See http://stfrancis
southfork.com/. (5-25-10)

Page 70, Emerson. See http://www.iwise.com/
XnirB. (5-25-10)